TRAINING YOUR BEST FRIEND

JOHN ROGERSON

ILLUSTRATIONS BY

McLACHLAN

STANLEY PAUL
LONDON

Stanley Paul & Co. Ltd
An imprint of Random House UK Ltd
20 Vauxhall Bridge Road, London SW1V 2SA

Random House Australia Pty Ltd
20 Alfred Street, Milsons Point, Sydney, NSW 2061

Random House New Zealand Ltd
18 Poland Road, PO Box 40-086, Glenfield, Auckland 10

Random House South Africa (Pty) Ltd
PO Box 337, Bergvlei 2012, South Africa

First published 1993

Set in Berkeley Old Style

Printed and bound in Hong Kong

A catalogue record for this book is available upon request from
the British Library

ISBN 0 09 177818 2

For my wife, Moira, the best trainer I have ever met.

Thanks to Julie Sellors, a specialist in contact learning, who
helped by writing Chapter 5.

CONTENTS

CHAPTER 1

COMMUNICATION SKILLS

For some reason I just can't get on the same wavelength as my dog

When we embark on a training programme, whether it involves highly specialised competition work or simply the creation of a well-behaved pet, the basic skills required to communicate effectively remain the same. If you are fortunate enough to watch several people with outstanding natural ability working with a dog (or any other animal) you will immediately notice that they have something in common: a feeling for the animal that they are working with. This is sometimes referred to as both dog and handler being on the same wavelength or being in harmony with one another. The people who experience difficulty in training are nearly always the ones who are not on the same wavelength and find themselves unable to communicate with their dog.

Many generations ago our forefathers were much more dependent on their domestic animals, for in some cases their very survival depended on an ability to understand and communicate with them. We ourselves have developed more and more methods of communicating with one another; simply by reading this book you are doing what is impossible for any other living animal. In writing it I am using symbols that you will form into words; you can then translate the words into pictures, limited only by your experience and imagination. The problem is, of course, that the more difficult I make the words and the sentences, the more I limit the number of people who are able to understand the book.

One additional problem that I am faced with is that I am writing in English, which means that if you only speak Japanese it makes no difference how simple I make the words, you will still not understand what I have written. Many people take the time and trouble to learn more than one language so that they are able to communicate with a greater number of people. For there is no universal language; or is there?

If you look at the illustration below, it makes little difference what country you come from or what language you have learned, you can still 'read' what the picture is saying. Music is also often referred to as the international language, because we can conjure up all sorts of mental images just by listening to a piece of music. Although the instruments may vary greatly from region to region, all music has certain components that are an indispensable part of its make-up. The language of music contains elements such as tone, timing and rhythm, balance and harmony.

The way that we use spoken language to communicate with one another is very different from the way that dogs communicate with one another. We use too many tones that sound the same, and too few pictures. A dog would use many more pictures and a small variety of tones. Included in the word 'pictures' are not only the visual clues that dogs use when communicating but also 'scent pictures'. When a dog sniffs and takes in scent he is able to conjure up pictures which will generate fear, expectation of food, excitement and images of other dogs and animals.

In order to communicate effectively with a dog and train him we must come to a compromise. We must teach our dog a basic understanding of our own spoken language and we must also be prepared to learn more about the language that our dogs use.

ELEMENTS OF CANINE COMMUNICATION

Sounds

When training a dog we often refer to the sounds that we make as COMMANDS. A command will tell the dog what action is expected of him, and so it is important that the sound chosen for each individual command is given in a consistent tone and volume and is sufficiently different from the sound of all other commands. This will mean that there is less likelihood of the dog misinterpreting commands that, to him, sound the same.

Signals

It is commonly recognised that it is perfectly feasible to train a dog by hand signals alone, without the need for any spoken commands. The one drawback with using signals is that the dog must be in a position where he can see the signal clearly. It is obviously not possible just by using hand signals to train a dog

to return to the handler when he is running away!

What is not generally recognised is the importance of the way that you are positioned when you are training your dog. Your dog will certainly pick up things like the way your feet are positioned, your hand positions, your head carriage, etc. This is known as body posture. If you study the illustration on page 9 you will quickly see that the person may be using the words "Come here", but the message the dog is receiving couldn't be more different.

Touch

Dogs will frequently touch one another to illustrate their intentions and to convey very strong messages. What is important is *where* dogs touch one another and *how* they touch one another. In the early stages of training, most handlers have no idea how to touch

their dogs; and for their part, many dogs assume that being touched on certain parts either constitutes a threat or requires an act of appeasement. The two best examples of this are: (a) the handler who tries to force a dog to lie down and finds that because of the apparent threat the dog starts to growl and stands even firmer, and (b) the handler who tries to get the dog to stand by lifting it up around the tummy and gripping its muzzle with the other hand, which usually results in the dog trying to adopt a submissive posture and lie down!

Smell

Few owners have any idea just how well developed their dog's sense of smell really is. If we compare our own sense of smell with an average dog we would find that the dog would be capable of detecting a smell that is one hundred times weaker than the most minute smell that we ourselves are able to detect. With training, and an above-average dog, the figure is much greater. Even though we recognise how good a dog's sense of smell

is, we seldom think about making use of this in order to reduce the stress of living in the 20th century.

Facial expression

Although this was partly covered in SIGNALS above, I wanted to place it in a separate category to underline the importance of facial expression in relation to training. Because our dogs are directly descended from the wolf, much of their behaviour and communication remains unchanged from that of the wolf. Wolves use a variety of facial expressions to communicate with one another, and we ourselves exaggerate our expression to make clear our intentions. The slight problem is that there is often a conflict between the two languages of facial expression. An open-mouthed 'smile' in dog language means "You're in trouble if you don't stop", whilst in human language the same gesture means "Hello, I'm friendly".

GOOD TRAINERS

Trainers that we describe as having lots of natural ability have simply learnt to communicate with their dogs using the languages that I have described above. A good trainer:

(a) Keeps all commands separate from one another, makes them clear and always gives each command in a consistent tone.
(b) Uses hand signals and body posture to aid the dog when teaching the commands.
(c) Knows when to touch the dog in order to help him into a position and when to leave him alone to move into that position by himself.
(d) Will have taught the dog to accept being touched and handled in a way that inspires confidence.
(e) Will have learnt to use facial expression to convey pleasure and displeasure and will have also learnt to combine this with both verbal and physical praise (speaking and touching).
(f) Speaks quietly and makes all movements steadily and deliberately.

(g) Never becomes bad-tempered or frustrated during a training session, as the display of either emotion induces stress in both dog and handler and is not conducive to learning.

(h) Never wears make-up when training, as this can easily over-emphasise facial expression.

(i) Wears comfortable clothing and shoes to aid natural body posture.

(j) Constantly observes or 'reads' the dog in order to anticipate the dog's next action and responds accordingly.

(k) Has the ability to time command, reward and occasionally correction so that the dog clearly understands exactly what is required.

(l) Will immediately be aware if the dog becomes confused and will offer support and reassurance when necessary.

CHAPTER 2

BEFORE YOU START

Many owners are fired with enthusiasm when they first start training, but that initial drive is soon lost when things begin to go wrong. This is often because they were badly prepared. In order to ensure that your training progresses quickly and easily we first need to take a look at the relationship that you should have with the dog that you are about to train.

Dogs are pack animals, just like their ancestor the wolf, and all pack animals need a leader. That should be where you come in. Your dog should look up to you and have some respect for your authority. This does not necessarily mean that you have to be the most dominant person in your household; but you should certainly hold a higher status than your dog. I know that as soon as I mention being dominant over your dog, this will create images of your having to shout, threaten or even get very 'physical' with your dog; but earning respect should not mean that your dog is forced to live under a dictatorship.

If we take a look at the way some dogs learn to become dominant over owners who fail to command their respect we can better understand how to exercise control over an already dominant dog.

HOW DOGS SHOW DOMINANCE

Sleeping/resting

A dominant dog will move another dog from its resting place whenever it feels like it, but no other dog can move *him* out of a favourite sleeping/resting spot.

Eating

Within a pack it is always the dominant dogs that eat first, particularly when food is in short supply. A dominant dog can also demand food from a more submissive dog that is eating, just by staring at it.

Playing

Dominant dogs are more interested in playing wrestling games and possession games that involve a lot of tugging against one another. It is during such games that dominant dogs learn that they are stronger than the rest because they control the games. This raises their status.

Grooming

A pack leader will often 'invite' selected dogs to groom him and will groom them back in return. A dominant dog will not allow a more submissive dog to approach and groom him unless he first invites the submissive dog to do so. Dominant dogs dictate all social inter-actions and they always begin and end such interactions.

Leading

Leaders lead: that is why a dominant dog will head a pack and not allow another dog to get in front of him. A dominant dog will always precede other dogs through doorways and into new territories.

WHO IS IN CONTROL?

If you allow your dog to eat before you eat, just because he demands it, and also allow him to demand the food that you are eating (some people call this begging), then he may begin to think that he is the one who is in control.

If he can also push you out of a chair or move you over in bed, whereas you find it difficult to move him out of a spot that he is occupying, then you will almost certainly have problems when you try to train him.

As well as this, if he plays lots of tugging games and always ends up with the toy at the end of the game, and if he loves to be touched on demand but is fidgety and difficult to groom, then you will find that when you try to train your dog he will constantly try to fight against your authority. If all of those things are true of your dog, then he is the one who is in control. He will therefore precede you through doorways and into new situations, seeing himself as your leader.

REGAINING CONTROL

If you are having problems in controlling your dog, then by eating before he eats at meal-times and refusing to give in to his demands for the food that you are eating you will begin to regain control and respect. In addition to this you can remove all toys and only play with your dog when *you* want to, putting the toy away at the end of the game in a place to which your dog has no access by himself. This, again, will give you more control, as you now have something that you can begin to use as a reward for the response that you require in training. You should also gain control of your dog's sleeping areas so that he is no longer allowed to push you off the chair on which you are sitting. For particularly dominant dogs it is also advisable to prevent their access to bedrooms. And finally you should make a point of teaching your dog to be groomed all over prior to going out for walks and before feeding. It also helps if you very occasionally (two or three times each week) ignore him when he demands to be stroked and petted. The importance of grooming cannot be stressed too much, as it is impossible to train a dog that will not allow you to groom him.

When your dog accepts all the controls I have mentioned, this will have increased his respect for you and it is now time to start training, provided that he is friendly and not nervous of other people or strange surroundings.

DOGS THAT ARE NERVOUS

Training a dog that is nervous of people will not improve his behaviour and could possibly make that behaviour worse by placing him under too much stress. When a dog is under stress he is not responsive: he is incapable of learning anything at all except how to escape from what is causing the stress. This means that your time is better spent socialising your dog than training him.

WHAT CAUSES A DOG TO BE NERVOUS OF PEOPLE?

Usually it is a lack of social contact with people at the critical phase of its development, which is between the ages of four and sixteen weeks. Or it may simply be that the mother was herself nervous of people and has trained her puppies to be frightened too. It is also possible that the young dog was subjected to a significant emotional trauma, such as being ill-treated by someone, and thus has developed a specific fear. To help your dog overcome his fears, the following programme is suggested. It should be completed before any formal training is carried out.

First list all the things that your dog really enjoys doing. Going out for walks, playing with a favourite toy and feeding are usually quite high on most people's lists, but feel free

to write down anything that causes your dog to become excited and wag his tail.

Now write the name of the person who is usually involved in most of these exciting activities. It is now a simple matter to ask that person to reduce the amount of their involvement in these favourite activities, and to start using other people that are known to the dog. Ask them to come and involve themselves more.

For the first week or so you could ask a friend, whom the dog knows, to come in and feed him every meal-time. For the second week try asking the person who was feeding the dog last week to take him out for some of his walks; then have another friend come in and feed him.

Each week try to include someone else in one of the activities that you have listed, and as your dog's confidence grows you can begin to introduce one or two people that your dog does not know quite so well. With care your dog should start to make the association between people and exciting things happening and should lose any fear that he may previously have had.

Once your dog becomes more confident in relation to people, then you can think about training him.

DOGS THAT ARE EASILY DISTRACTED BY OTHER DOGS

It is a difficult and frustrating affair to attempt to train a dog that is continually being distracted by the presence of other dogs. If we take a look at the main reasons for a dog being more interested in other dogs than he is in his owner, the logic behind my suggestions for improving the relationship between dog and owner will become clear.

Dogs, remember, speak the same language. It is therefore understandable that they will be keener to exchange information with one another than to try to communicate with their apparently deaf owners. Imagine moving to a foreign country where you do not speak the language and where there is no one to teach you. Then imagine the attraction of meeting someone who comes from your own country and can speak your language.

When a dog is completely distracted by another dog the choices are: (a) to teach your dog a little of your language; or (b) to learn a little of your dog's language; or (c) to do both.

Most dogs that are easily distracted by other dogs have one thing in common: a desire to play with one another. For the majority of dogs this represents the highlight of their day, simply because the owner does not play enough with them; and even when they do, these human games lack excitement.

It is also quite often the case that the dog that is easily distracted in fact lives with another dog. This means that the bond between the two dogs is stronger than the bond between dog and owner.

If you own more than one dog, then try

Stay!.... I mean... Wuff!

this simple test. Leave one dog in the house and take the other out for a walk. When you return to the dog that you have left in the house, watch to see which of you it greets first: you or the other dog. Now swap dogs and repeat the test. What most people find is that one of the dogs will greet them first, but the other will greet the other dog first. It is no coincidence that this will be the one who is easily distracted by other dogs.

To resolve the problem, all you need to do is to spend some time on a worthwhile session of play with your dog and his favourite toy, generating as much excitement as you possibly can. If you own more than one dog, then you must limit the amount of free play that they have with one another and play with them individually; then they will both get more enjoyment out of playing with you than they do from playing with one another. This now means that when other dogs are around, you yourself are the biggest distraction in the area. Never punish your dog for wanting to go up and say "Hello" to another dog, but use this desire to your own advantage by teaching him to obey a simple command or two before giving him your permission to go and see the other dog.

When calling him away from other dogs, always reward the behaviour that you want by using a toy or treats; and after rewarding him, occasionally allow him to return to the other dog for a few minutes.

As soon as you have reduced the attraction of other dogs you can begin your dog's more formal training programme.

AGGRESSIVE BEHAVIOUR

If you are experiencing any problems where aggression is involved then you should consult your vet before you start training. Some behaviour problems are due to medical causes which your vet can treat; or you may possibly be referred to a pet behaviour therapist who specialises in the treatment of behaviour problems.

The Association of Pet Behaviour Counsellors is the only professional body in the U.K. that specialises in the treatment of behaviour problems and will see clients only on veterinary referral. The letters A.P.B.C. after the therapist's name are your guarantee of a high standard of service.

CHAPTER 3

AIDS TO TRAINING

Learning how to use and apply the many aids to training that we have is something that is often completely overlooked, and yet it can make such a difference to the speed at which a dog learns to carry out a command. In this chapter we will examine these aids in detail so that you are much more aware of how they can be applied to your training programme.

YOUR HANDS

You will often find it necessary to use your hands in training in order to move and manipulate your dog into some of the positions required. You will also have to use your hands a great deal in order to stroke and make a fuss of your dog (physical praise). It then makes sense that before you start any training you should ensure that your dog accepts both being moved around by your hands and also being stroked by them. Unfortunately some dogs, instead of having a pleasant association with their owners' hands, have been smacked, threatened, grabbed or pushed around by them; so the associations are sometimes unpleasant. It is also a fact that many dogs then become difficult to train because they have developed 'hand shyness'.

YOUR VOICE

We all use our voices to talk to our dogs, but in training you will need to use your voice effectively so that your dog clearly understands what you are asking him to do. Your voice will also reflect your emotional state: so it is important to be in control of your emotions before, during and immediately after a training session. Your ability to change the tone of your voice to generate excitement,

encouragement and approval, as well as disapproval, will make all the training sessions much easier for your dog to understand. Resist the temptation to prolong a training session if you become frustrated, and never attempt a training session if you are in a bad mood.

FACIAL EXPRESSION

Smiling can be very effectively used either by itself, if your dog needs a little reassurance, or in conjunction with both physical and verbal praise. With a very sensitive dog, changing from a smile to a frown can be extremely useful as a means of showing disapproval in order to correct an unwanted response. Learn to smile pleasantly when you use the words "good dog" and it will sound to him as though you actually mean it! You should also learn to frown if you change your tone from very pleasant to mildly unpleasant.

THE LEAD

Your dog's lead is one of the most fundamental items of training equipment, but it is also one that few owners give a lot of thought to when purchasing this essential aid. Even when the correct lead has been purchased for training it is often used incorrectly.

Most dogs have a pleasant association with their lead because it is often linked with the excitement of going out for walks, whilst a few dogs have an unpleasant association because they have experienced what it feels like to be smacked with it.

For training purposes your lead should be either a flat leather one or alternatively one of the cotton/nylon types that are now readily available. The width of the material will be dependent on the size and strength of your dog, and it should be long enough so that when your dog is standing alongside you, the lead hangs loosely underneath his collar. When you measure this length you should have the hand that is holding the lead at the

height of your waist. This means that you can drop your 'lead hand' if you need to give your dog a little more freedom, and by raising it you will take up all the slack to restrict his movement. If the lead is too long you will be forced to use two hands on it in order to take up the slack, while if it is too short there will be far too much tension on your dog's collar when he is walking with you. The clip on the lead should attach to the collar so that when you are walking, the attachment point is underneath and not on top of the dog's neck.

THE COLLAR

There is a bewildering assortment of collars available for the dog owner to choose from, and although most of the collars are sold as being designed to give greater control, few actually do this. If you successfully teach your dog to pull against you in an ordinary collar, then the chances are that you will be equally successful in teaching him to pull in a half-check collar, a choke chain, a head-collar or any other anti-pulling device.

For training purposes choose a flat leather or nylon collar that has a buckle for adjustment purposes; the width of the collar will

depend on the size and strength of your dog. To make sure that you obtain a collar of the right size, place a piece of string around your dog's neck, high up under the ears, and tighten it so that you can get only one finger between string and neck. Now remove the string and measure it. Choose a collar whose middle adjustment hole approximately corresponds with the length of your piece of string.

FOOD

Never underestimate the use of food as a reward in training: many of the tasks that we require our dogs to learn can be made easier and more enjoyable if food is used correctly. For food treats to be of benefit, your dog should see them as something special which has to be earned rather than being his by right. This means that all food used in training must be used sparingly and all training must be timed to take place prior to feeding time. To increase the effectiveness of food in training you can use portions of your dog's daily diet rather than giving treats which are additional to his meals.

Remember that if you use food treats in addition to plenty of verbal and physical praise, then not only can you increase the effect of the reward but you can also eliminate any dependency that your dog has on treats during training. If food treats are used correctly, your dog should carry out your instructions for you in the hope of receiving a reward rather than doing what he is told just for the treat alone.

GAMES

Almost every pet dog loves to play games, and you can make use of this in training, first of all by learning to understand what games your dog likes to play and then by picking a toy that you can use to excite and play with him. Games are usually easier to manage if you use a specially designed training toy rather than using yourself as a toy. The advantage of using a toy is that you can put it away when you have finished, in order to maintain your dog's enthusiasm for play as a reward in training. Never leave your training toy around for your dog to play with unsupervised: he may either destroy it or else lose interest and become bored.

When you use a toy as a reward be sure to include lots of exciting verbal and even physical praise to maximise his enjoyment. Remember that the excitement has to be generated by you; it is impossible to force a dog to play.

OBSERVATION

Observation is one of the most useful but least used aids to training that we have at our disposal. If you give your dog one hundred per cent concentration whenever you are training you should quickly begin to be able to predict what he is likely to do next. By being able to predict his next movement you will be in a position to time your reward so as to maximise its effect. It is sometimes helpful to go along and watch other people training their dogs so that you can build up your powers of observation. If, for example, you are watching a dog being trained to do a sit stay and he continually breaks this position you should begin to notice a pattern. The dog may, for instance, look away from the handler and glance back to them just prior to moving. If you can predict this behaviour in your own dog, then you are in a position either to prevent him from looking away by focusing his attention on you, the handler, or to apply some mild verbal correction just prior to his movement and then to reward him for staying. Good trainers are invariably excellent observers of the dogs they are working with.

CHAPTER 4

PRE-TRAINING

In order to prepare yourself and your dog for training you will need to learn the following exercises to make the whole learning process as easy as possible.

CONTROLLING THE REWARD

Before you can use a reward effectively you need to learn how to control its use. Ideally your reward should produce some degree of excitement; but over-excitement can be just as counter-productive as no excitement at all.

Stroking
(physical praise)

Try stroking your dog gently, without speaking, when you are calmly seated in your own house: note the degree of excitement that this creates. Now begin stroking more enthusiastically and watch to see how excited he becomes. If you get to the point where he starts jumping up, out of control, or begins to do a wall of death around the furniture then you are over-exciting him. The balance that we are looking for is when he becomes excited but not uncontrollable.

Speaking
(verbal reward)

Once you have tried the stroking test, you should repeat the experiment by talking in a pleasant tone and noting your dog's reaction. Increase the excitement in your voice to test how much excitement you can generate in your dog: too much, and you lose control, too little, and you will fail to get a reaction at all.

Speaking and stroking
(physical and verbal praise)

By combining these two methods of reward you should find that it becomes easier to over-excite your dog, particularly if he already has an excitable nature. You will need to learn how to use and combine these aids so that you can generate excitement without losing control. The amount of reward will obviously vary greatly with each individual dog; that's where your powers of observation come in.

FOOD

There is not much point in using food as a reward if your dog is aggressive when he is eating, or if he becomes so excited that he snatches food out of your hands.

If you are going to use food treats, then master this pre-training task first. Begin by holding a treat between your finger and

thumb and attract your dog's attention. Bring the treat down to within an inch or two of your dog's mouth; do not allow him to touch it. If he tries to snatch it out of your fingers, do not pull your hand out of the way but frown and use a stern tone of voice until he gives up trying to take it from you. After he has waited patiently for a few seconds you can smile and use a really pleasant tone as you allow him to take the treat. Most dogs learn really quickly that they will not get the treat if they try to grab at it but that they will get it if they wait patiently for it to be offered. If your dog continues to be aggressive when food is around, then it would be wiser to forget about using food as a training aid and rely on praise and toys.

TOYS

Toys are one of the most successful aids to training that we have at our disposal, but they are also one of the most misunderstood aids. Before you can attempt to use toys it is vital that your dog learns the correct set of rules for the games that you are going to play. There is not much point in throwing a toy for your dog as a reward when training him to come to heel off the lead, if he then picks it up and runs away with it. If this happens, you will probably spend more time trying to get your dog to come back to you with the toy than you will spend in teaching heelwork. Similarly, if your dog likes to grip the toy tightly between his teeth, making it difficult to get it back from him, you will not be able to use this form of reward until you have more control over these games.

Before using toys as a reward you should first teach your dog to retrieve the toy you have thrown for him. This can usually be

accomplished by attaching a length of line to your dog's collar and using it to draw him back towards you. Always remember to praise well BEFORE you take the toy away from him to throw again. If your dog tends to snatch at the toy when you are holding it, then you can use the technique described above for preventing the same behaviour

over food. If there is a problem in getting the toy out of your dog's mouth then you will need to be very patient. Encourage him to give it up and wait quietly for him to do so. When he releases his grip and lets you take the toy, you should then praise and reward him for letting go. Sometimes a correctly timed food treat will help.

ATTENTION AND CONCENTRATION

Dogs vary greatly in the length of time that they are able to concentrate. You should be aware of how long your dog can maintain concentration, so that in the early stages of

training you do not take him beyond his present limit. If a training session drags on for too long, it all becomes rather counter-productive and often results in the trainer becoming frustrated.

To work out how long your dog's span of concentration is you can try this simple attention exercise. Using either a toy or a food treat, go into a room where it is quiet and there are no other people, pets or any other distractions. Sit quietly alongside your dog and get his attention fixed on the reward that you are using. Do not actually let him touch the reward, but use your voice to encourage him to concentrate on the food or toy. Time how long it is before he begins to lose concentration, give him the reward and then repeat the exercise another four times in quick succession. The average length of time

that you were able to hold your dog's attention on the reward will be the maximum length of time that you should spend on teaching each exercise when you begin your training programme. With practice you can dramatically increase your dog's ability to concentrate and therefore his ability to learn what you are trying to teach him.

Dogs that are often referred to as hyperactive seem to have little or no ability to concentrate on anything for more than a few seconds at a time, whilst dogs that have been very highly trained are often capable of concentrating for twenty minutes and beyond. The more you repeat this attention exercise the better your dog will become at concentrating. Remember that if you cannot get your dog to concentrate on the reward in the comfort of your own home where there are no

distractions, then it is pointless going out to training classes or into a public area to train.

HANDLING

Training a dog invariably involves a degree of physical handling; so it is as well to teach your dog to accept being handled as a pre-training exercise.

Begin by attaching a lead to your dog's collar, and either fasten the free end to something sturdy or get someone to hold it. This leaves both your hands free. First pick up each of his feet in turn, beginning at the front. Remember to praise and reward as soon as your dog allows each foot to be moved. Now ease your dog into the lying-down position and roll him over on his side.

Coax and encourage him as much as possible until you have the desired response. Now gently roll him over onto the opposite side and reward him when you have done so. Finally get him to stand up from the lying-down position by enticing him with your reward, then turn him around in a half circle so that he is facing the opposite direction, then turn him back again. If at any stage you meet with any resistance, do not progress beyond that point until he accepts your moving him. It will help considerably if you combine this exercise with daily grooming (just as important if you own a smooth-coated breed) prior to taking your dog out for walks, feeding him or playing with him. If daily handling sessions become associated with a pleasant experience, then the dog should soon look forward to being handled.

CHAPTER 5

CONTACT LEARNING

Contact learning is a new, holistic approach to animal health and training. As we have seen from the previous chapters, touch is an important part of communication between dogs and ourselves. A dog learns much about his surroundings through touch, and this, combined with physical contact with his litter-mates, also teaches him co-ordination and control in his movements. Developing this body awareness helps his confidence and his ability in relating to other animals and acquiring the skills needed in later life. If the dog is deprived of the comfort and stimulation of physical contact he will fail to thrive and will not fulfil his potential, either physically or emotionally.

Enormous benefits can be gained by improving our touch communication and developing a dog's confidence and control in his own movements. There are also benefits to us: touching reduces our blood pressure and heart-beat rate and is a natural way to ease emotional and physical stress. It can even save you money! When systematically touching your dog you may find swelling, heat or pain that would otherwise have gone unnoticed. This can then be dealt with at an earlier, less complicated, stage by your vet. Also, because your dog is accustomed to being touched, your vet will be able to handle him much more easily - vital if he needs emergency treatment.

By using simple, gentle touches rather than absent-minded stroking we can increase the effect of touching a pet. Here some gentle touches are described; but before starting, give your dog an overall assessment. Study him to get to know how he moves - how does he hold his head and tail? Does he move in straight lines, or slightly sideways when viewed from front or rear? Is there a lot of movement in his back, or do his legs move under him without causing such movement? Has he a long, flowing stride or a short, choppy one? Is his stride length regular, or is one leg put down after a slightly shorter movement? Do his legs move in a straight or a circular movement? How does he sit, stand and lie down? Being familiar with your dog and analysing his movement helps you to know if something is wrong. Many times you may have said "Something is not quite right with him today", but by learning to watch your dog you will know when this is so. As you become more aware of your dog's usual movements you will be able to pinpoint the 'not quite right' area. Remember, when you study your dog, that even dogs of the same breed can move very differently. What you need to find out is what is usual for your dog.

TOUCHING YOUR DOG

I refer to touch rather than massage because when massage is mentioned it conjures up thoughts of deep muscle massage that uses quite a lot of pressure. This requires an extensive knowledge of anatomy, as the pressure that is applied could cause discomfort and even damage to the dog if done incorrectly. The type of touch described in the following text is very light and works on the cells and nervous system.

Start by practising on yourself and you will then experience the effects from your dog's point of view. When you are comfortable with your ability at controlling the speed and pressure of your touch you can gently begin on your dog.

When working on your dog it will help you to concentrate and your dog to relax if you choose a quiet, warm room away from other pets. Do not restrain your dog, for if he walks away it is because he isn't comfortable with what you are doing! Speak in a quiet, reassuring voice. Breathe slowly and deeply, and start on an area that is acceptable to him. Always be gentle, and gradually you will be able to continue for longer periods of time. Never continue to the point where he becomes bored, as this will lead to his resisting your touch and tensing up - the very opposite of what you want to achieve. It can take time to build up the trust and confidence needed to work through the routine, but when this trust is achieved it deepens the relationship between you and your dog.

A good opening touch to get your dog relaxed and ready for more contact is a quick, light, flicking motion against the direction of hair growth. Using a relaxed, cupped hand gently go over the body as if flicking off dust. This touch is ideal for fidgety or touch-sensitive dogs. After a few seconds of this you can move on with your hands in a raking shape

(the heel of your hand and fingertips in contact with the dog) and make long strokes. Start under your dog's tummy and work up towards his back. Your dog should now be settled and ready for the next stage.

With one hand lightly resting on your dog, use the flat of your other hand gently to push the skin around in circular movements. Start off quickly, and then gradually slow your breathing and your hand movements. As you slow down, be very aware of your breathing; concentrate on making single circles and feeling the skin sliding over the top of the muscle.

Do this randomly all over your dog's body, and use only enough pressure to slide skin over muscle. Gradually work towards the more sensitive areas, such as the paws, then gently spread the toes and work between the pads. At any time you can gently slide your dog's ears between your fingers and thumb. The ear contains all the acupressure points of the body, and by these gentle sliding actions of the ear the whole body is affected.

As you get more practised, experiment with different light touches. Some dogs find finger-tip contact very pleasant, but others may find it too invasive. Watch your dog's face and body and be sensitive to any changes; remember, this is something which should be pleasant for your dog.

Then with the flat of his hand he pushes the skin round in circular movements

If your dog finds any of the touches too invasive try lightening the touch, or using a sheepskin pad. This is really appreciated by short-haired or sensitive dogs.

When you have finished, gently make long strokes over the whole of the body to join up all the areas that you have been working on.

IMPROVING CO-ORDINATION

For dogs who have difficulty in focusing their attention (concentrating) or appear to be clumsy (lack of body awareness and control)

the touch work can be combined with ground exercises. The ground work is similar to the exercises young horses are taught to improve their balance and co-ordination, and it consists simply of a series of obstacles that the dog is walked over. The touch work, combined with ground exercises, improves and develops the dog's co-ordination and body control. These exercises are simple, are fun, take very little time, give a deeper appreciation of your dog's ability to learn quickly and aid team work in your general training. The touch and ground work exercises release tension and reduce stress and so help the learning process. People and animals learn more if they are relaxed and enjoying themselves.

Old tyres and plastic pipes are ideal obstacles; they are cheap, easily obtainable and practically indestructible. All you need to do is to lay some of your obstacles on the floor in a random pattern and lead your dog through them. If your dog trips over the tyres or pipes use a stick to tap the ground in front of him and draw his attention to them. Another method to assist learning is to use food treats in front of your dog so that he lowers his head and sees them. At first he will probably try to leap the pipes or roll them over, but after a few attempts he will learn how to step over even the most complicated obstacles. This will increase his confidence and his adaptability in new situations. When leading the dog over the obstacles try not to use the lead to control him. Let him find his own balance and control. Dogs that have done a lot of obedience work are often only worked on the left of the handler and can become very one-sided. In order to counteract this, ensure that you lead him over the obstacles from both sides. Be patient, and also watch where you put your feet. Often if you are careless your dog will be, too; but if you pick your feet up well clear of the obstacles your dog will mimic you and clear them more easily. Take the obstacles slowly and deliberately and give your dog and yourself time to think about what you are doing.

Combining the touch and ground exercises will help improve your dog's learning ability, and because you will develop a greater awareness of your dog's feelings and abilities, it will make you a more effective and understanding trainer.

CHAPTER 6

THE RECALL EXERCISE

Because this is one of the most essential and basic of all exercises, it is always the first one that we teach. Most owners make the mistake of trying to teach the exercise outside rather than in their own home, assuming that the dog will come readily and consistently when they call him in his familiar environment. Before you start any training outside, you and your dog should both pass the following simple test. If you fail, you will need to begin at stage one; if you pass, you can begin at stage two.

THE TEST

This is divided into five sections, and you must repeat each section once. You must not advertise that you have a reward available before you test your dog, although you may give a reward if you are successful at the completion of each test. You are only allowed to give your dog's name and recall command ('Come', 'Here', etc.) once; repeated commands constitute failure of that section of the test.

(1) When your dog is in the same room as you, but not paying any attention to what you are doing, call him to you and hold onto his collar. You are not allowed to move towards him, apart from extending one arm. He should come to you readily and willingly. If he refuses to come, or ignores your command, or if you have any difficulty in getting hold of his collar without moving from your position, you have failed.

(2) When your dog is in the next room to where you are, and completely out of your sight, call him to you and hold onto his collar when he comes close enough. The same rules are used as in section (1) above.

(3) When your dog is in your garden (only if you have an enclosed garden or yard), stand in the house, out of sight, and have a lead ready. Call your dog and, when he comes to you, clip the lead onto his collar before you reward him.

(4) When a family member or friend comes into your house, allow your dog to run up and greet them. Position yourself as far away from your dog as is possible, bearing in mind that you should remain in full view. Tell the person to stand still and not speak to your dog. Now recall him, and when he comes close to you, hold onto his collar before rewarding him.

(5) Have a friend or neighbour bring in another dog. This must be a dog that has a friendly, outgoing temperament and preferably one that your dog already knows and is friendly with. The other dog should remain on the lead throughout this test. Let your dog run up and greet the other dog, and after about two minutes call your dog. Use the same conditions as in section (4) above.

HOW DID YOU SCORE?

If you scored 0 out of 10 (each section was repeated once, remember), this would suggest that your relationship with your dog is not good enough to enable you to begin training. This score is most frequently seen in owners who have more than one dog, the

bond between the dogs being stronger than the dogs' bond with the owner. So if you have a dog that is not at all responsive to you, then you will have to start by rebuilding your relationship before you can begin training.

If you scored between 1 and 5, this indicates that your dog is responding to you when there are no distractions, but also that he has to date received little if any formal education.

A score between 6 and 9 would indicate that there is a specific recall problem, such as your dog not wanting to have a lead clipped on or being too much distracted by the presence of other dogs or people, or both.

The minimum pass mark is 10 out of 10. If you cannot get your dog to return to you immediately in your own house, you will not have the amount of control necessary to attempt to train him in the exercise outside where there are likely to be many more distractions.

If you were unable to undertake one or more of the sections because you have a problem with your dog's temperament, then this should be corrected before any training is carried out.

STAGE ONE TRAINING

This is for dogs and owners who scored less than 10 out of 10 in the test above. Try to have a clear idea in your mind of what you are teaching before you begin each session so that you know the goal that you are trying to achieve. You should also remember the aids to successful training and use them throughout.

Begin by having your dog in the same room as you are, and have a reward readily available. Get your dog's attention by calling his name in an excited tone of voice. Try to resist the temptation to raise your voice. When your dog has his attention on you, show him the reward that you have on offer and then use your chosen command to call him towards you. Remember to smile and use your voice to encourage him to come closer. When he comes within reach, do not grab at his collar, but touch it gently with one hand whilst you give the reward and stroke him with the other hand. You can repeat this part of the exercise several times, depending on how long your dog is able to concentrate. It is better to do one or two recalls ten times each day rather than ten recalls once per day.

If your dog does not come to you instantly after you have been training him for several days, then you will need to understand what is going wrong. Failure to recall at this stage can be neatly divided into three main problem areas. By observing what your dog does when you try to recall him you should be able to establish what you need to do next in order to gain the desired response.

Problem One

When you call your dog he approaches, but stays just out of reach and goes into a 'freeze' position. His eyes fix on a position just slightly to your right or left and he lowers the front of his body slightly, wagging his tail. What he is doing is 'inviting' you to chase him! The slightest movement that you make results in his racing away or past you, just out of arm's reach. I understand just how frustrating this is, but you must remember that he is only doing what you have trained him to do by chasing him around.

To correct this problem, you should attach a length of cord to his collar before starting a training session. Let him drag this around; do not hold onto it. Ignore your dog and walk past him until you are in a position where you can step on the line. Now when you call him and he comes to you, kneel down and gently draw in the excess slack. When your dog goes into the 'freeze' position, make a slight movement backwards, away from him. Keep your foot on the line so that he is prevented from running away or past you. Now coax and encourage him to come closer. Be

away and avoid direct eye contact, his ears will be laid back and he may even lick his lips. There are two possible reasons behind this behaviour: either the owner has called the dog to chastise him more often than for a reward, or the dog is naturally submissive and feels overpowered by the signals given off by his owner.

The cure for this problem is the same in each case. Change the command that you use: it may already have slightly unpleasant associations. 'Come here' may be changed to 'In', 'Close' or 'To me'. When you give the command, remember to sit or kneel on the floor, open your arms invitingly and smile. When your dog comes close enough, gently caress or stroke him before giving a food treat. Try to keep your voice soft and encouraging and, above all, be patient. Each step that your dog takes towards you should be rewarded, even if it is only one faltering step at a time. Until your dog is consistently returning happily, avoid calling him when you are standing up.

patient and refuse to allow your dog to turn this into a game. Smile and use all your aids to get him to approach; frown and change the tone of your voice slightly if he tries to avoid you. Never try to hold the line and haul him in: this will simply teach him to come when you are holding onto a line and he will soon learn to ignore you when the line is not attached.

Problem Two

When you call your dog, he approaches and slows up until he comes to a complete stop just out of reach. As he approaches, he looks as though he is under stress, with his tail tucked underneath him, and his tail wags stiffly from side to side. He will also look

Problem Three

When you call your dog, he takes absolutely no notice of you, sometimes not even bothering to look round at you. This usually occurs in dogs that have learnt to be independent and have been desensitised to their names. This means that the owner has repeated the dog's name on a daily basis, over and over again, without attaching any meaning to it. The dog's name then simply becomes background noise and, like the sound of the washing machine or the central heating boiler starting up, it is totally ignored.

To correct this problem you will need to attach a length of cord to your dog's collar and let him trail it around in the house, provided that there is supervision at all times. Wait until he is unaware that you are behind him, and then pick up the line, call his name using a touch more urgency in your voice and give your command at exactly the same time that you give a sharp flick with the line. This flick is designed to convey to your dog the message 'I'm talking to you'. It is not intended to shock or cause any discomfort. The instant that your dog looks at you, immediately show your reward and encourage him, using all possible aids, to come towards you.

When your dog is reliable at coming when called, you can begin to include out-of-sight recalls from one room to another, and you can also include some distractions. Always remember to increase your reward if your dog has any difficulty in learning any of the steps, and never try to progress beyond the rate at which your dog is able to learn.

STAGE TWO

This stage is used when your dog scores 10 out of 10 in the recall test in the house. Go out to a completely enclosed and safe area free of distractions, first making sure that dogs are permitted access. Fasten a long line onto your dog's collar for safety and then remove the lead. Allow him to wander away and, when he gets somewhere near the end of your line, put your foot on it and recall him. Do not hold on to the line or pick it up at any stage; it is merely attached to prevent your dog from running off and getting too far away from you. The length of this line will depend on how far away you want your dog to exercise from you.

Use all your aids to get your dog to return and, when he does so, clip the lead on before rewarding him. Then remove the lead and repeat the exercise several more times. When you do your final recall before returning home, make sure that it is not carried out in the same spot each time within your training area, so that your dog cannot predict when the lead is about to be put on to take him home. What your dog should learn after a few sessions is to come when called for his reward, and to have his lead put on. He will also learn that having the lead put on is not going to curtail his freedom in any way.

When you are satisfied with his response you can begin to include distractions, just as you did at home, until you are confident enough to remove the line in the knowledge that you have complete control over your dog. It now helps to improve your dog's response if you start to REDUCE the number of rewards that he gets at each session so that you keep him guessing as to which recall is going to produce the reward that he wants.

CHAPTER 7

WALKING ON AND OFF LEAD

There can be few worse sights for a trainer to watch than someone being dragged along the street by their pet dog. It is not only uncomfortable for both the dog and the owner but it is also totally unnecessary. When a dog pulls on the lead he becomes completely unbalanced: in fact, he is only able to remain upright because of the pressure that the owner is exerting on the lead in the opposite direction. Because the dog is so unbalanced the owner becomes unbalanced and has to alter the whole of their body posture in order to compensate. This means that they quickly become tired. There is also the distinct possibility that the dog may even manage to pull them to the ground, particularly if it is wet or slippery underfoot. The reason that most dogs pull on the lead is simply because they have no desire to walk alongside their owners. This usually occurs because there is little incentive for the dog to walk correctly and plenty of incentive for it to pull. Think, for instance, of a walk to the local park: the dog gets excited and pulls on the outward journey because it is anticipating the reward of free exercise when it arrives there. After exercise it walks back home in a much more balanced fashion and hardly pulls at all, because there is little incentive to do so.

Whatever the reason, the problem is that as soon as the dog begins to get ahead of the owner, they immediately put pressure on the lead in an attempt to keep the dog next to them. As soon as this happens, the dog has to put exactly the same amount of pressure on the lead in order to counteract the pressure applied by the owner. As the dog is pulled back into the heel position, the owner is applying more pressure on the lead: the dog attempts to counteract this by leaning forward. In order to lean forward he must drop his head and extend his neck, and at the same time lower his centre of gravity by bending and opening his front legs. When the owner has managed to pull the dog back into a position alongside them, they reduce the pressure on the lead. This results in completely unbalancing the dog, whose centre of gravity is now so far forward because of his posture that the only way that he can prevent himself falling over and regain his balance is by surging forward. This causes the owner to tighten the lead and repeat the whole process all over again. Just to make matters worse, some owners then begin to use a word of command such as 'Heel' which the dog interprets as 'Brace yourself: I am about to try and pull your head off'!

There are three basic techniques that you can use, depending on whether you are wanting to train a puppy or to correct an older dog that has already started pulling on the lead. You will need to decide which is the more appropriate method for your dog.

METHOD ONE

This is used for young dogs as part of their formal education and can be started as soon as your dog is used to wearing a collar in the house and is able to go outside. Place the dog in your car and drive a short distance away from your house. One hundred yards is a good distance at which to start. Place the dog on the pavement and begin walking back towards your house. If the dog starts to lag behind, you should try to coax and encourage him by offering a reward. Resist the urge to pull your dog along behind you; this will only make him brace himself against the pressure that you are exerting on the lead and pull backwards away from you. When he is walking alongside you, use your voice and

hand aids continually to reward him. If he surges ahead, do not pull against him. Take a quick pace forward and put pressure on the lead in a forward direction: i.e. pull him forwards. Your dog's immediate reaction will be to pull backwards against the pressure of the lead and return to the correct position alongside you. Remember to reward well when he is walking correctly. If he puts any pressure on the lead you should apply pressure in the direction in which the dog is travelling. Do not put on pressure in the opposite direction, as this will only encourage him to pull harder

to resist you. Obviously, you can only use this technique for puppies and young dogs, and you will need to use one of the other methods for a confirmed puller. As your dog gets the hang of what is required, you can begin to increase the distance you walk back home. When you are confident that your dog is walking without pulling, then you can walk him from home to your car, parked a short distance away from your house. After this has been accomplished you can then walk him out to and back from an exercise area where he can be allowed some free running exercise.

METHOD TWO (THE SNAPPING LEAD)

This is easier to describe if you imagine that you are holding the lead with two hands, although in practice it can easily be accomplished with just one. With your dog on your left, hold the handle of the lead in your right hand. Your left hand should be positioned on the lead so that your dog has only about two feet of movement in any direction. Now walk forward and wait until your dog begins to exert a small amount of pressure on the lead held in your left hand. As soon as you feel any pressure, stand still, let go of the lead with your left hand and give a sharp flick with your right hand. When your dog is standing upright and alongside you, praise him well before you continue walking. Repeat as necessary in order to teach him to want to walk alongside you. The whole process, from your dog putting pressure on the lead to the point where you are praising him

for being in the correct position, should take no longer than two seconds. From your dog's point of view, it should seem that every time he exerts pressure on the lead, it breaks. As he is then slightly unbalanced, he will stumble forward and hit an invisible wall. The idea, of course, is not to harm him in any way, or even to cause him any discomfort, but merely to teach him not to trust the lead as something to lean against.

METHOD THREE (THE ABOUT TURN)

This method relies on putting pressure on the lead in the direction that the dog is pulling and also stopping all forward progress, putting him in a position behind that of the handler. This is a particularly useful technique for a dog that pulls hard on the outward journey and walks home reasonably well.

Hold the lead in one hand and allow plenty of slack between yourself and your dog. Have your dog positioned on your left and walk forward in a straight line. As soon as your dog gets in front and begins to exert even the slightest pressure on the lead, smartly right about turn on the spot and put pressure on the lead. Your dog should now find that he is positioned directly behind you. It is now time to increase the pressure on the lead as he comes towards you to try and catch you up. Because you are now pulling him forwards, he should resist this pressure by pulling backwards, which is exactly what you are trying to teach him. You will need to be very patient and persistent when using this method, as at first you will find that you make little forward progress. As your dog begins to understand what is required, you must remember to increase your rewards when he is walking as you want him to. A correctly timed food treat will speed up the learning process.

When you are satisfied that your dog will consistently walk on the lead without pulling, you can begin to introduce a command of 'Heel', 'Close' or 'Watch', etc., each time that you move away from a stationary position.

Before you attempt the exercise off the lead (on a quiet walk, away from livestock and traffic), it is a good idea to toss the lead over your shoulder so that you still have control of your dog if necessary but you also have both hands swinging freely by your side. It is important to note that no matter how well your dog is trained, you should never walk a dog off lead anywhere near a public highway: apart from being a very dangerous practice, it often constitutes an offence.

Whilst you are using any of the above techniques to teach your dog to walk correctly it will be of benefit to teach the ground exercises described in chapter 5. These exercises are aimed at improving your dog's natural balance and control, an essential element in walking on the lead.

CHAPTER 8

DOWN, SIT AND STAND STAY

Teaching the stay exercises will really test your powers of observation to the full. The more observant you are, the easier it is to train your dog to remain in one position until you give him your permission to move. The first difficulty that we encounter is actually to get the dog into the desired position; the second difficulty is to teach him to remain there.

TEACHING THE THREE POSITIONS

Sit

Begin by attaching a lead to your dog's collar. If he is a small dog you may find it easier at this stage to lift him onto a raised platform or table. Stand with your dog in the stand position on your left-hand side and get him to fix his attention on a reward held in your right hand. Now speak his name and give the command 'Sit', and at the same time raise your right hand (with the reward in it) so that it is just above and slightly behind his head. You may need to help him into this position at first, either by gently pressing on his rump with the flat of your hand or alternatively by touching his hind legs with your arm to 'tuck' his hind legs into the sit position. As soon as he is in the correct position, immediately reward him, making sure that he does not move from that position. After rewarding him for a few seconds, stop all rewards and allow him to move by giving him a 'break' command such as 'Free' or 'Off'. Repeat the exercise several times but remember not to exceed his concentration time, which by now should be several minutes. When he will go into the position on your command alone, without the need to touch him in any way,

then you can progress by teaching him to sit from the down position. First, though, you have to teach the down position.

Down

Start with your dog alongside you on your left and in the sit position that you have previously taught him. Place your right hand with a reward in it just in front of your dog's nose. Now slowly lower your right hand to the floor between your dog's paws, encouraging him to follow it with his nose. When his nose is close to the floor simply slide your hand forward, using his name and your chosen command such as 'Down', 'Lie' or 'Flat'. You may find it necessary to place your left hand on his shoulders so that you can gently push and assist him into the position. As soon as he is lying down, allow him to have the reward, but remember to keep him in this position for a few seconds whilst you praise him before releasing him with your 'break' command. Continue training as you did for the sit position until your dog will

readily go into the down position by following your hand and without the need to touch him. Now you can think about training him to go into the down position from the stand. First, though, you have to teach the stand.

Stand

The easiest way to teach the stand position is by walking your dog into it from the sit position. Begin with your dog in the sit position on your left and hold a reward in your right hand at the same level as his nose. Now move the reward forwards and encourage your dog to follow it, helping him into the stand position by gently pulling forwards on the lead and giving the 'Stand' command. As soon as your dog is in the stand position you should place your left hand just inside his hind leg to ensure that he stays in this position whilst you reward him. After several seconds of praise you can give him your 'break' command and allow him to move.

If you train all three commands in the above sequence until your dog is familiar with them and moves into them readily without assistance you can then progress by teaching him how to move into any position from any other position.

When your dog can go into the sit from the stand you can teach him to go into the sit from the down by starting off with him in the down position and then holding a reward above and behind his head and giving the 'Sit' command. It sometimes helps if you gently tickle the front of your dog's feet either with the side of your foot or with your hand. Reward as soon as your dog makes an effort to sit.

To teach the down from the stand you simply begin with your dog in the stand posi-

tion and move your reward swiftly to the floor between his front feet, helping him by gently rocking him backwards with the lead. Reward as soon as he is in the required position.

To teach the stand from the down you can use the same technique that you used to teach the stand from the sit.

By the time that you have reached this stage your dog should willingly move from one position to another with the minimum of assistance and should do so readily and eagerly. You can now begin training him in the stay part of the exercise.

TEACHING THE STAY

Begin with the lead attached, so that you are in total control of your dog. Place him in the desired position with your command and then move to a position directly in front of him. Whether or not you use a command of 'Stay' as you move is unimportant, as you have already taught him to remain in that position until you give your 'break' command. However, most people still choose to use the command of 'Stay'. Now watch him intently. Talk to him and reward him gently with your voice all the time that he remains in the stay position. Remember to keep smiling. You should be able to keep your dog in this position and maintain his attention just by your tone of voice and your facial expression. Too much excitement in your voice, and he will get up and come towards you; too little, and he will lose attention and concentration. If your dog moves, you should quickly change the tone of your voice and your facial expression and also note what he did immediately before he moved. Quickly place him back in EXACTLY the same spot and repeat the exercise; but this time try to look out for the warning signs that show he is about to move, and correct him with your voice alone before he does so. Keep speaking and smiling all the time that he remains in the correct position. Only expect to keep him in the stay position for a few seconds and then return to him and reward him before giving your 'break' command. Never finish the exercise by calling him towards you, as this will only encourage him to move instead of staying until you return to him, which is the whole point of the exercise.

As your dog begins to understand what is required you can gradually increase the time that he is required to stay until you can easily get him to remain for two minutes. You can now progress to moving further away, first by dropping the lead on the floor and then by detaching it altogether.

Remember that the exercise always finishes with you returning to your dog and not with your dog returning to you. It sometimes helps if you mark the spot where you want

your dog to remain by placing a piece of tape, or even a lead, on the floor directly in front of him. If you have learnt to use tone of voice and facial expression correctly you can very quickly teach your dog not to step over the line that is placed in front of him.

As your dog's understanding of the exercise improves you can start to train using some distractions and then progress to training outside. For safety, all early stay training outside should be carried out on a line. You should also make sure that if you leave your dog in a stay position outside a shop or anywhere near traffic, he is on a lead and the lead is securely fastened to some convenient point.

CHAPTER 9

FURTHER TRAINING

Once both you and your dog have mastered all the basic control exercises, a whole new area of training opens up to you both. There are of course many specialist training classes and groups where you can both go and advance your capabilities. These range from competitive obedience classes, which are similar to dressage, to working trials, which are like a three-day event, although you normally only work on one or two days. There are also fun competitions, such as agility, which is similar to show jumping, and flyball, which is a new sport where dogs compete in relay teams over a set of low obstacles, retrieving a ball from a specially designed box in the process. However you decide to advance your training, the principles that you have applied in teaching your dog the basic exercises will still apply.

The process by which a dog learns is governed by a few simple rules, which you have already learned to apply in teaching the control exercises.

RULE 1

If a behaviour is rewarded it will tend to increase in frequency.

This means that when your dog obeyed a command to sit, for example, he received a reward immediately. After a number of repetitions he would associate your command 'Sit' with the action of moving into that position in order to get the reward.

RULE 2

If an action is not rewarded it will tend to decrease in frequency.

Remember when you taught the recall exercise? If your dog was one that went into the 'freeze' position ready for you to begin a game of chase, you were asked to attach a line to his collar. Then you were in a position to control the dog and prevent him from turning the exercise into a rewarding game of chase. Because he no longer had the reward of a game of chase, this behaviour became less frequent.

RULE 3

If a behaviour produces a negative response it decreases in frequency very rapidly.

When you trained your dog in the stay position, you would have used a pleasant tone of voice all the time that your dog remained in the desired position. When you thought he was about to move you changed your facial expression and also the tone of your voice to let him know that his impending movement met with your disapproval. This should very quickly have stopped him moving, particularly as he was receiving a reward for the behaviour that you wanted.

RULE 4

When a behaviour has been fully learnt, if it is then rewarded at random, that behaviour dramatically increases.

This is why you were asked to reduce the number of times that you rewarded your dog after it had fully learnt and understood the recall exercise. I suggested that you 'keep him guessing about which recall is going to produce the reward that he wants'. If you think carefully about this rule you will realise that it is the reason why people learn to gamble. It also explains why gambling, for some people, can become an obsession!

All your training to date has concentrated on teaching a dog how to respond to one simple command which required a single action on his part. But how about if you want to train your dog to carry out a more complex task that requires more than one action on his part? The first thing to do is to break the exercise down into small segments, each of which can be taught separately. Arrange these segments in their logical sequence and write them down. Now you will need to understand about 'reverse chaining'.

REVERSE CHAINING

This simply means that we are going to start training the dog in the last segment of the exercise first so that he gets rewarded for finishing it. Once your dog has learnt the last segment we then teach the second last segment, and when he has learnt that we add it to the previous one, and so on until the dog has learnt the whole task. This sounds very complicated in theory but is easier to explain in practice. I have picked a complex exercise so that we can examine the various stages that are required to teach it. The exercise is to teach the dog to smell a handkerchief and then to run into a small area of dense woodland and to find the person who owns the handkerchief. When he finds that person he must sit next to them and bark to let his handler know that he has located them.

Breaking this exercise down into small segments would be done as follows:

(1)   Train the dog to smell a handkerchief.
(2)   Train the dog to explore a dense wood.
(3)   Train the dog to ignore anyone to whom the handkerchief does not belong.
(4)   Train the dog to find the person to whom the handkerchief does belong.
(5)   Train the dog to sit next to the person he has found.
(6)   Train the dog to bark whilst sitting next to the person he has found.

We now have six segments, all of which are going to be relatively easy to teach. We begin with the last segment (6), and then when the dog has learnt that part we add the next (5), and so on. Try it for yourself and you will be amazed at how quickly your dog can learn.

Begin by getting a friend to hold a reward such as food or a toy just in front of your dog. Have your dog in the sit position, on the lead, and get your friend to call and encourage until your dog makes any noise at all. Immediately your dog makes a noise, tell

your friend to reward him instantly. After several repetitions, reward only when your dog actually barks and ignore all other noises that he makes. When your dog understands that it is the action of sitting and barking that brings him the reward that he wants, you can introduce a command of 'Find him', just before getting your friend to excite him.

Now hold your dog at a short distance away from your friend. Release your dog with your command and when he gets to your friend, ask them to use the command 'Sit'. Your dog should sit and then, with very little encouragement, begin to bark for the reward that your friend is holding. Continue training until your dog runs to the person and sits and barks of his own accord, without requiring any prompting.

You can now let your dog sniff at a handkerchief belonging to your friend before releasing him to run a short distance to bark. Each time, increase the distance a little.

The next stage is to have two people standing several yards apart. Let your dog sniff a handkerchief belonging to one of them. Release him with your 'Find' command and allow him to run up to your two assistants. If he barks at the wrong one they are simply to ignore him (behaviour that is not rewarded decreases in frequency). When he chooses to sit and bark at the correct person they must immediately reward him (behaviour that is rewarded increases in frequency).

When your dog is consistently locating the correct person you can then position them close to the edge of a wooded area. Stand well away from this area and then ask your assistant to attract your dog's attention. This person should then run into the woods and stand just out of sight behind the first tree that he comes to. Send your dog to find them with your 'Find' command. When your dog enters the wood he should have little difficulty in finding and barking at your assistant.

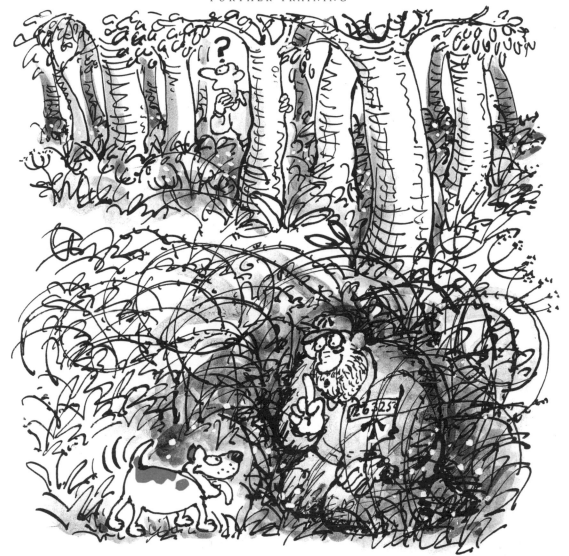

The last stage is to position two people in the woods; the dog should be familiar with both of them. One of these people will have your dog's reward, and this person should have given you their handkerchief. Let your dog sniff the handkerchief and send him out into the woods with your 'Find' command. By now your dog should understand that he is to search the woods until he finds the person who smells the same as the handkerchief. When he locates that person he will immediately remember to sit next to them and bark for the reward that he knows will be given for this behaviour.

You should remember that it will be impossible to teach this exercise unless you have first trained your dog in all the control exercises. The more control that you have over your dog, the easier it becomes to train him in the more complex tasks.

How long should it take to teach this exercise? A dog that learns fairly quickly, plus a good trainer, should take about five 10-minute sessions, spread out over a two-day period! If you now understand the basic rules for training and the concept of reverse chaining, you should have little difficulty in training your dog to carry out any advance task.

CHAPTER 10

GAMES AND PARTY TRICKS

It is amazing how many dogs we see where owners have very little control over them when they are out for exercise, but which can perform the most amazing repertoire of party tricks. I can recollect watching a young lady working her dog at a dog club progress test. The dog performed really badly and she complained that she was unable to get its attention fixed on her. She described the dog as being easily distracted, wilful and disobedient. After the test the handlers were asked to demonstrate any party tricks that their dogs could perform. The young lady who had been having all the problems in the test promptly won the party tricks section with one of the most amazing demonstrations I have ever watched. The dog rolled over on command, gave first one paw, then the other paw and then both paws. He also lay 'dead' on his back when she pointed at him and said 'Bang'. She asked him to add up several numbers and he barked the correct answer. He walked backwards, sat up and begged and caught and retrieved dog biscuits without eating them. When I spoke to her afterwards she said that her dog always enjoyed party tricks, and gave her perfect concentration because he would do anything for a reward. It's strange how so many people think about using rewards when they teach party tricks but stop using rewards and begin to use compulsion when training their dogs in control exercises.

When you start to teach a party trick you will generally be more relaxed, because the outcome is not really critical. This in turn means that your dog will be more relaxed and better able to learn. You will also see this as more of a game and less of a formal exercise, and so your dog will enjoy the training sessions more. If you find that your dog learns party tricks more quickly and easily than the formal control exercises you will have to re-examine your approach to training.

The following suggestions are offered in order to encourage you to explore the full range of skills that your dog possesses, and to test your skill as a trainer who truly understands your dog.

BELL RINGING

Teach your dog to ring a bell when he wants either to go out into your garden to relieve himself or to let you know when he wants to come back into the house. The bell can be a mechanical one that he rings by pulling on a cord with his teeth, or it can be a battery-operated one that works when he presses a button with his paw.

FIND THE LADY

This is a simple card trick that exploits your dog's sense of smell. Place three cards face down on the floor, one of which is the queen of hearts (it helps if this card also happens to smell of liver!). Tell your dog to 'find the lady' and let him locate the correct card and indicate this by pawing at it.

CLOSE THE DOOR

When you enter the house, go into a room, leaving two interior doors open behind you. Send your dog to close them in sequence so that he ends up in the room with you.

HIDE AND SEEK

Teach your dog to find a member of the household who has been allowed two minutes to go and hide anywhere in the house. All room doors are to be left open, unless you can teach your dog to open doors as well!

NAMED RETRIEVE

Line five of your dog's toys up on the floor and ask him to bring you the ones that you name in sequence. For a more advanced version you can place all the toys in an open box and ask him for each one in turn.

And now here are three tasks that will test your skills as well as those of your dog.

COLOUR BLINDNESS

Devise a test for your dog to determine whether he is able to see and distinguish between the following colours: yellow, red, green and brown.

FIGURE OF EIGHT

Stand to one side and teach your dog to do three consecutive figures of eight around two chairs placed five paces apart.

Please remember that if you do not manage to train the dog in some of these tasks it is not the end of the world. Dogs have different levels of skills and a task that one dog can carry out with ease may prove extremely difficult for another.

THE END

Now that you have finished reading this book, teach your dog to place it back in the magazine rack or on the coffee table.

Well, it's not really the end because training doesn't have an end; learning is a continuous process which starts the moment your dog is born. The reason we own pet dogs is because they enrich our lives. A well trained dog is a pleasure to own whilst an untrained dog is often a liability. Which would you prefer to own and to share your life with?

I hope that I have conveyed the feeling that training your dog is fun and rewarding for you both. But please do not take my word for it: instead, go and try it for yourself. A wealth of informative material has been published on this new, kinder approach to training, and your local library should have a reading list that will keep you going for several weeks or even months. I have included a recommended reading list at the end of this book in case you want more information or more challenging tasks to teach your dog.

If you become interested in competing with your dog, then you should contact the Kennel Club. They will send you details of the various types of competitions that are licensed in England, Scotland and Wales. Your local veterinary surgery and animal welfare kennels are also good sources of information about training classes in your area.

At present there are no minimum requirements for anyone who runs a dog training club, and so standards do vary greatly from region to region. It is always wise to go along and check out a training class to ensure that the methods used are acceptable to you and your dog. Of course, there is always the prospect of learning more about training and then starting up a club yourself, to help other owners get the best out of their best friends.

RECOMMENDED READING LIST

YOUR DOG
Its Development, Behaviour and Training
John Rogerson

UNDERSTANDING YOUR DOG
John Rogerson

TRAINING YOUR DOG
John Rogerson

BE YOUR DOG'S BEST FRIEND
John Rogerson

THE FAMILY DOG
Its Choice and Training
John Holmes

USEFUL ADDRESSES

THE KENNEL CLUB
1 Clarges Street, Piccadilly, London W1Y 8AB

ASSOCIATION OF
PET BEHAVIOUR COUNSELLORS
257 Royal College Street, London NW1